AMAZING SCIENCE

ARMADILLOS

AND OTHER

UNUSUAL ANIMALS

Q.L. PEARCE
Illustrated by Mary Ann Fraser

Julian Messner

To Kristina

Acknowledgment

With thanks to Rebecca Hudson, Public Information,
Los Angeles Zoo, for her critical reading of the manuscript.
I would also like to thank Yvonne Maizland, docent at the
Los Angeles Zoo, for her assistance.

Library of Congress Cataloging-in-Publication Data
Pearce, Q.L. (Querida Lee)
  Amazing science : armadillos and other unusual animals / Q.L. Pearce ;
illustrated by Mary Ann Fraser.
    p. cm.
  Bibliography: p.
  Includes index.
  Summary: Brief introductions to thirty animals with unusual and bizarre
habits—such as the hognose snake who plays dead as a defense mechanism
and the sand skink who can see through windows in his eyelids.
    1. Animals–Miscellanea–Juvenile literature. [1. Animals–Miscellanea.]
I. Fraser, Mary Ann, ill. II. Title.
QL49.P34   1989   89-9315
591–dc20   CIP
                                        AC

ISBN 0-671-68528-7 (lib. bdg.)
ISBN 0-671-68645-3 (pbk.)

Contents

The Animal World

Have you ever heard of a lizard that squirts blood at its enemies, a fish that sleeps in a cocoon, or insects that use their own larvae to "sew" leaves together? There are more than a million different kinds of animals in the world. From one-celled microscopic creatures to the mighty elephant, each type of animal has its own special and sometimes surprising features and behavior. A characteristic that seems very strange to us may be just the thing that helps the creature to survive.

The giant anteater, for instance, uses its strange long snout and sticky tongue to get its food. It eats a huge amount of ants and termites, which often live in hard-to-reach places. The anteater's snout is just long enough to reach the insects, and its tongue is particularly well suited for the task of collecting them.

Lots of animals also have bizarre ways of escaping from their enemies. A predator that catches a glass-snake lizard by the tail will be surprised to see the rest of the animal wriggle quickly away. The hognose snake, on the other hand, doesn't try to get away at all. Instead, it tries to confuse its attacker, first by imitating the behavior of a poisonous snake, and then by pretending to be dead.

Some animals have unique traits that help them to survive harsh climates, from freezing Antarctica to the hot Sahara. For example, the hairy-nosed wombat must adapt to the deserts of northern Australia, where water is scarce. The animal does this by getting all its moisture from its food. The hairy-nosed wombat doesn't have to drink at all.

This book will introduce you to these and other amazing inhabitants of the vast world of animals.

The Aardvark

Shortly after sunset, a most peculiar-looking animal trots out of its burrow on the African grasslands. With its long, rabbitlike ears and piglike nose, this creature looks like a character from a fairy tale. It also has a peculiar name, *aardvark* (ARD·vark), which means "earth pig" in the Afrikaans language of South Africa. This animal is between four and five feet long, not counting the tail, and weighs between 175 and 220 pounds. Although it looks like a large barnyard pig, it is not related. In fact, the aardvark is in an order all by itself because of its unusual teeth. Each tooth is filled with fine tubes but has no enamel and no roots.

The aardvark is an excellent burrower, because the toes of its front feet have strong, sharp claws. Balanced on its hind legs, the aardvark shovels soil away with incredible speed. It scoops out tunnels that join in a large underground sleeping chamber.

Termites are this creature's favorite food. With its sturdy claws the aardvark can easily rip open a termite mound, then poke its sticky eighteen-inch-long tongue into the nest and lap up hundreds of insects. It doesn't mind the termites' bites and stings–the aardvark's skin is tough enough to protect it. The aardvark can also close its nostrils so the insects can't crawl inside.

Other hungry prowlers, such as pythons, hunting dogs, and lions, may attack the aardvark while it is searching for food. But the aardvark is not helpless. If trapped, it rolls onto its back, kicking and scratching with its dangerously sharp claws. If it has enough warning of danger, it can disappear very quickly into the ground. The amazing aardvark can dig a hole faster than a person with a shovel can.

At dusk, the aardvark scurries out of its
burrow and begins its nighttime prowl.

The African Lungfish

How long do you suppose you could survive without food or water? The remarkable African lungfish can survive for as long as four years! It has adapted to the harsh climate of central Africa in a special way. During the rainy season, when the climate is mild and damp, the lungfish usually eats earthworms, tadpoles, and small frogs. Using the two rounded teeth in its upper jaw and several teeth in its lower jaw, the lungfish sucks in, crushes, and chews its prey. But when the dry season comes, and drought dries up the lakes or swampy places where it lives, the slender, six-foot-long lungfish doesn't eat at all.

As the water disappears, so does its oxygen supply. This doesn't bother the remarkable lungfish, however. Swimming to the surface, it opens its mouth and sucks air into its pouchlike lungs. If the pool dries up even further, the lungfish sinks into the mud. It burrows a long tube, wider at the bottom, so that it can turn. This astonishing fish folds itself into a "U" shape with its head and tail turned toward the surface. To keep from drying out, it covers itself with slimy mucus. The mucus hardens into a leathery cocoon with a very small opening or tunnel to the surface. Mud hardens around the cocoon, sealing the fish inside. Scientists have found ancient cocoons with fossil lungfish inside that are at least 180 million years old.

While in the cocoon, the lungfish doesn't eat. It lives on food stored in its body. To save energy, its heart beats more slowly. The fish sucks air from the tunnel down into its lungs. When the rainy season begins again, the rain softens the mud and fills the ponds and lakes. Once again, the lungfish swims free and breathes with gills like any other fish.

While in its underground cocoon, the
African lungfish will not eat or drink.

The Arrowpoison Frog

A most unusual family of frogs lives in Central and South America. Called arrowpoison frogs, this family includes the smallest frog in the world, the one-half-inch-long *Sminthillus limbatus* (smin·THIL·us lim·BAT·us). This group also includes some of the most beautiful frogs. Most have brilliantly colored patches and swirls of red, black, green, blue, or yellow. The bright colors are a warning to other animals: These tiny frogs are quite deadly when eaten.

All arrowpoison frogs carry a very strong poison on their skins. The local Indians dipped their arrows in this poison to kill their prey. To find the tiny creatures, the natives would imitate their call and listen for answering chirps. The frogs were pierced with a stick and then held over a fire until droplets of poison formed on the skin. When rubbed over a frog's back, grooves in the arrow tips picked up and held the poison. The strongest poison comes from the little one-inch-long kokoi (koh·KOY) frog from Colombia, South America. It may be the most powerful poison known. One-thousandth of an ounce is enough to kill a human.

Would you think such poisonous frogs would make good parents? Actually, the male arrowpoison frog is a very good parent. When the female lays her eggs, the male attaches them to his back with sticky mucus. After the eggs hatch, he sometimes carries the young tadpoles on his back until they are quite large. During that time, he will occasionally take a dip in water to soak the young and keep them moist. The offspring also get moisture from the tropical rain. When the tadpoles become too large for the father to carry, he takes them to water and they swim away.

*The tiny arrowpoison frog is beautiful—
but deadly poisonous.*

Blind Salamanders

Salamanders look a lot like lizards, but unlike those reptiles, they do not have scales or claws. They are *amphibians* (am·FIB·ee·ans), which in Greek means "double life." Amphibians are so named because most live at least part of their lives in water and part on dry land. There are about 350 different kinds of salamanders. Like most other amphibians, they lay eggs that hatch into a tadpole stage. As tadpoles, they live in water and breathe through gills. As adult salamanders, they live on land and breathe with lungs.

Blind salamanders are very unusual. They never leave the tadpole stage, and they don't need good eyesight since they live in the dark waters of shadowy caves. The ghostly pale Texas blind salamander lives in the dark, muddy streams and deep wells of the Purgatory Creek system in Texas. The only entrance to the home of this phantomlike cave dweller is called Ezell's (EE·zellz) Cave. Its only visitors are thousands of bats that roost on the cavern's damp ceiling. The Texas blind salamander is an odd-looking animal with tiny, weak legs, a flattened snout, pink ruffled external gills, and undeveloped eyes. This salamander has no use for eyes— it finds the worms and shellfish it eats by smell.

Most amazing of all, perhaps, is the grotto salamander of the Ozark Mountains. It begins its life in open streams as a typical salamander. It has true eyes, external gills, a large tail fin, and brown skin. As it enters its adult stage, however, it loses its tail fin, gills, and skin coloring, and retreats into the darkness of a cave. No longer of any use, its eyes stop growing and are covered over by skin.

Living deep inside Ezell's Cave, the Texas blind salamander has no need for eyes.

The Burying Beetle

Believe it or not, nature has a special "cleanup crew" all its own. When a very small animal dies, the tiny black-and-orange burying beetle often picks up the scent and flies in to bury the body. If the dead animal is not lying on loose soil in which to bury it, the one-inch-long beetle will actually move it. First it sends out a chemical signal for help from beetles of the opposite sex. Several may arrive, but only one will stay with the beetle who sent the signal to do the cleanup work. One insect crawls under the dead animal, turns on its back, and pushes the body with its tiny legs, moving it slightly. The two beetles take turns doing this job over and over again until the carcass has been moved to a suitable burial site. The insects dig the soil out from under the dead animal until the body falls into the pit and is covered by loose soil.

Why do the burying beetles go to all that trouble? The answer is to feed their young. In a short tunnel above the burial chamber, the female lays about fifteen eggs. When the beetle eggs hatch, a fine meal is waiting for them. When strong enough, the new young adults tunnel out and fly away.

The burying beetle has another odd feature. It almost always has little companions. Dozens of tiny pink spider mites cling to its back. In the burial chamber, the mites help the beetle. They eat any fly eggs on the dead body. Because of this, hungry fly maggots that could compete with the young beetles for the food don't hatch. The mites also reproduce in the same chamber, so when a young beetle leaves the chamber, it is already covered with helpful young mites.

*The burying beetle can bury animals
many times its own size.*

The Collared Peccary

According to an old tale, the collared peccary (PEK·uh·ree) has two navels, one on its belly and one on its back. The truth is even stranger. The "navel" on its back is actually a special gland that secretes a liquid that smells strongly of musk. The desert animal rubs the smelly fluid on rocks, tree trunks, and even other peccaries. The scent both marks the animal's territory and helps peccaries to recognize each other.

Another unusual fact about the peccary is that it is also known as the javelin (or javelina for the female) because of its strong spearlike upper teeth. Sometimes males threaten each other with a peculiar rattling noise made by chattering their sharp teeth. The peccary's strange teeth are also very handy in eating the incredibly wide variety of food in its diet. The peccary may have a meal of mice, lizards, and insects, or it may gobble down fruits, roots, and tubers of desert plants, including prickly pear cactus. Sometimes this odd creature even eats a little soil, perhaps to get minerals that it needs in its diet.

The collared peccary can run quickly. It uses its speed not so much for hunting but to escape from the jaguars and pumas that are its enemies. But if one of these predators attacks a whole herd, the peccaries do not run off together. Barking in alarm, they all run in different directions, which often confuses the enemy. When in such danger, all members of the herd protect the young. If babies are with the herd, one adult peccary will bravely risk its own safety and turn deliberately toward the attacker to draw its attention. This gives the rest of the herd a chance to get away.

To confuse an attacker, the collared peccary barks in alarm.

The Duck-Billed Platypus

When the first stuffed specimens of the duck-billed platypus (PLAT·ih·pus) arrived in England from Australia, most people were amazed at the sight. Some thought the animals were fakes made by sticking parts of different animals together. It's easy to see how they made that mistake, because this is a very unlikely looking creature. It has a wide, flat muzzle like a duck's bill, ducklike webbed feet with sharp claws like a cat, and short brown fur and a wide tail like a beaver.

The platypus is indeed a very special animal. It is a monotreme (MON·oh·treem), an egg-laying mammal. About two feet long from bill tip to tail, it weighs about five pounds. It eats shrimp, worms, and tadpoles, which it must crush with the horny plates in its strong bill. The male has spurs on its hind feet. The spurs contain a poison that can kill some small animals and be very painful to a human. The platypus is one of the very few poisonous mammals.

The duck-billed platypus makes its home in quiet waters with muddy bottoms. Digging into the soft riverbank, this small burrower builds a complicated system of tunnels with entrances above and below the waterline. The platypus spends most of its time in the water. The webbing on its front feet extends beyond its claws to make excellent paddles. On land, the webbing folds under for walking or digging.

To prepare for her offspring, the female platypus builds a small nest of grass and leaves in the burrow. Here she lays two or sometimes three eggs and incubates them for about two weeks. The female eats a lot before she lays her eggs, because she does not eat during the incubation period.

The strange-looking duck-billed platypus—
part duck, part cat, and part beaver.

The Echidna

Imagine a walking pincushion and you will have a good idea of what the echidna (eh·KID·nuh) looks like. Coarse hair and long sharp spines cover its rounded body. When alarmed, this strange little animal can roll up into a prickly ball. Its long spines protect it from predators.

Like the duck-billed platypus, the echidna is a monotreme. It lives in Australia, New Guinea, and Tasmania. Unlike the platypus, however, the echidna doesn't build a nest. The female usually lays one egg a year, which she keeps tucked safely in a temporary pouch on her belly. The baby hatches in about ten days, but it stays in the pouch to develop further. When the baby grows spines, it becomes uncomfortable for the mother to carry. Finally, she puts it in a safe hiding place and returns every day for about three months to feed it until it is old enough to take care of itself.

The echidna is nocturnal. That means it hunts at dusk or at night. It waddles slowly, scratching the ground for food, sniffing all the while with its long snout. It has good senses of hearing and smell but poor eyesight. Digging with its strong curved claws, the echidna roots in the ground for ants, termites, grubs, and beetles. In fact, it is sometimes called the spiny anteater. Because it has no teeth, the echidna laps up the scurrying insects with its long tongue.

The echidna's body temperature may vary slightly with its surroundings, more like a reptile than a mammal. The echidna hibernates during the cold winter. When the weather warms in spring it awakens, sheds its spiky coat, and grows a new one.

If you see a walking pincushion,
it is probably the echidna.

The Gharial

Do you ever wonder how creatures from the age of the dinosaurs really looked when they were alive? Actually, the modern gharial (GAR·ee·ul) looks almost exactly like its ancient relative, the phytosaur (FY·toh·sore). The phytosaur was a large reptile that lived in swamps and along muddy riverbanks more than 200 million years ago. The gharial is also quite large and may grow to a length of twenty feet. It swims in the large muddy rivers of northern India: the Ganges (GAN·geez), Indus (IN·dus), and Brahmaputra (bram·uh·PEW·truh). There is one very noticeable difference between the two creatures, however. The phytosaur's nostrils were near its eyes at the beginning of its long snout, but the nostrils of the gharial are at the end of its long thin snout.

The gharial's jaws are lined with about a hundred small, sharp teeth. By sweeping its head back and forth in the water, the gharial catches the fish it eats. Although it doesn't attack humans, this huge reptile will feed on dead bodies put in the Ganges River after funeral services.

There is some confusion over this strange animal's true name. The gharial was originally named for the rounded, cuplike tip of the male's snout. The word *ghara* in the Hindi language means "pot." However, this relative of the crocodile is more commonly known as a gavial (GAV·ee·ul). That's because in an early story about the gharial, a clerk made a mistake when copying the text and misspelled the name. People now use the incorrect name more often than the correct one.

The twenty-foot-long gharial is a relative of the ancient phytosaur.

The Giant Anteater

The incredible giant anteater may gobble 30,000 insects in a single day. This gigantic appetite has earned the anteater a nickname—"the ant bear." As you might suppose, insects make up most of this creature's diet. It usually hunts during the day, finding its meal by scent. The giant anteater's very long, toothless snout is equipped with a two-foot-long tongue covered with sticky saliva. As its tongue captures ants and termites, the anteater's tough, leathery skin and eyelids protect it from their painful bites. This creature also uses its long, curved claws to dig and to rip open termite nests. To protect these useful claws, the anteater must walk on its stout knuckles with its fingers curled under.

The giant anteater may be six to seven feet long, but more than half of that length is in its bushy tail. The clever anteater has found many uses for its very long tail. When resting under a log or in an abandoned burrow, the anteater curls up and covers its eyes with the tail. It also uses it to sweep insects from its coarse fur.

This unusual animal lives in the swamps, humid forests, and grasslands of Central and South America, from Guatemala to northern Argentina. Unlike its relatives, the lesser anteater and the two-toed anteater, it does not climb trees. Instead, it strolls slowly along, with its long nose to the ground sniffing and searching for a meal. Sometimes the giant anteater will run into one of its natural enemies, the speedy puma or the powerful jaguar. It will usually try to run away. Although it gallops clumsily, it can usually escape fairly quickly. If forced to fight, however, the razor-sharp claws of the giant anteater can deal a dangerous blow.

The giant anteater can break into a termite
nest and eat thousands of the insects.

The Glass-Snake Lizard

Is it a snake or is it a lizard? As its name might suggest, at first glance it's hard to tell what the glass-snake lizard is. Because its slender body has no legs, it looks very much like a snake. But unlike a snake, this creature has eyelids that can blink. The answer to this riddle is that the glass-snake lizard is . . . a lizard.

Although the "glass snake," as it is commonly called, does resemble a snake, if you look for certain other features you will be able to identify it as indeed a lizard. Snakes, for example, do not have ear openings, but this creature has small, round ear openings just behind its eyes. Also, when you hold the glass-snake lizard, it feels more like a lizard than a snake. That's because the animal's smooth, shiny scales are reinforced with bony plates, making its body feel stiff compared to that of a snake. The glass-snake lizard has another remarkable feature that no snake has. Slender grooves along each side of its body expand when the animal is eating or laying eggs.

This unusual reptile lives in dry grasslands and open woodlands. Insects, small lizards, snakes, and young mice make up its diet. The glass-snake lizard's tail is almost as long as its body. If you frighten the animal, it will try to slip away. But if you capture it and, instead of holding the body, you grab its tail, an astounding thing happens–the tail breaks off at the base and splinters into several pieces. It seems to shatter like glass. Without its tail, the lizard can now make good its escape. A new tail will grow, but the break will always be visible.

If you grab a glass-snake lizard's tail, it will shatter to pieces.

The Gnu

Because of its wild leaps, twists in the air, and other crazy antics, the gnu (NEW) is known as the "clown of the Serengeti." It lives on the grasslands of Africa. Grazing herds of gnu, also called wildebeest (WILL·duh·beest), may number in the thousands. During the dry season, smaller herds move together between watering holes. When the rains come again the animals are more scattered.

The appearance of the gnu seems strange, and its body seems out of proportion. This animal looks like it has the body of a horse, the head of a broad-nosed ox, and the slender legs of an antelope. The front end is much stockier than the hindquarters. Stiff black or white hairs form a raggedy beard, a long mane, and tufted tail. Both males and females have a pair of curved horns.

At breeding time, aggressive males stake out tiny territories, some no more than a few feet wide. At the center of the territory is the bare "stamping ground." Here the male spends most of his time, head held high, tail swishing. He performs a complicated display of ownership not only of the territory, but also of any females passing through it. He runs in circles, prancing, tossing his mane, and kicking high up into the air. These amazing acts are accompanied by a combination of snorts, coughs, and bellows. The gnu certainly does a lot to attract a mate.

Eighty percent of gnu calves are born during a three-week period in January or February. A calf can stand within a few minutes after birth and is able to run beside its mother within thirty minutes. Although lions, cheetahs, and wild dogs kill hundreds of calves, so many gnu are born at once that enough survive to keep the gnu population plentiful.

The strange-looking gnu has the body of a horse and the head of an ox.

The Hairy-Nosed Wombat

Have you ever heard of an animal that carries its baby around in its pocket? The hairy-nosed wombat does. Like kangaroos and koalas, it is a marsupial (mar·SOO·pee·ul), or pouched mammal. The female has one baby at a time, which she carries in a pouch on her tummy. Since the pouch opens toward the rear, sort of like an upside-down pocket, dirt is kept out when the mother is digging.

Wombats dig a lot, in fact. People have even nicknamed this animal "the marsupial bulldozer." You've probably never seen a bulldozer that lies on its side to work, but that's what the hairy-nosed wombat does. It scoops out the soil with its front feet and pushes the dirt away with its hind feet. This small animal digs a network of tunnels, where it can rest during the heat of the day. When the weather is cool, it sometimes comes up to sunbathe, but usually it surfaces at dusk or at night.

With front teeth like chisels, short legs, and a stub of a tail, the rare hairy-nosed wombat looks like a cross between a rodent and a small, chubby bear. It makes its home only on the coastal plains of southern Australia. Usually little fresh water is available in this warm, dry area. That doesn't bother the wombat, however. The water it needs comes from its food so it doesn't have to drink at all. Its teeth grow continuously and must be worn down by gnawing. This it does by chewing on tough bark. The wombat eats only a few types of plants, but when it finds one it likes, it may gobble down the whole thing—roots, leaves, bark, and all.

The hairy-nosed wombat—nicknamed
"the marsupial bulldozer."

The Hognose Snake

If you come across a hognose snake in a field, it will probably do its very best to scare you. When surprised or frightened, this clever reptile imitates other, more dangerous snakes. It begins the act by flattening its neck, raising its head, and hissing like a cobra. Next, it opens its mouth threateningly and lunges at its attacker as if to bite. But the hognose snake is just an imposter, a harmless mimic. In fact, it doesn't even bite.

If the performance doesn't frighten away the attacker, the snake has another trick. It suddenly rolls over in convulsions and seems to die right on the spot. You can even pick it up and it will still play dead. If you put the snake back on the ground, right side up, it will flip back over into its deathlike position. This, too, of course, is an act. After a moment it will very slowly turn and peek to see if the enemy is gone. If not, it will "die" again.

The hognose snake goes into convulsions in order to protect itself from predators. Or does it? Actually, some scientists think the snake behaves so peculiarly because of its diet. The animal lives in open fields, prairies, and wooded hillsides, where it finds the toads it loves to eat. However, it is known that a certain species of toad it eats is mildly poisonous. Some scientists believe that when the snake is frightened, the poison it has eaten takes effect, causing the animal to go into convulsions and collapse. If this is true, then the bizarre behavior of the hognose snake is not an act after all. This remarkable reptile may actually faint with fright.

The hognose snake has all sorts of
tricks to scare away attackers.

The Jackson Chameleon

If you picture an animal that has horns, you might think of a bull or perhaps a rhinoceros. But would you ever picture ...a lizard? The five- to seven-inch Jackson chameleon (kuh·MEEL·ee·un) is just such a creature. It has three impressive horns projecting from its head. These horns are important in battles over mates. The male uses the horns not so much to hurt a rival, but to push it off its branch. The female has horns too, but they are hardly noticeable.

Chameleons are the quick-change artists of the animal world. Most, including the Jackson chameleon, can actually change the color of their scaly skins. Special cells in the Jackson chameleon's skin can shift in size very quickly. These cells are different colors, such as black, white, and yellow. As black cells expand and white and yellow ones shrink, for example, the chameleon appears to darken. Changes in temperature or in the animal's mood will cause a change in color. The lizard may brighten when excited, darken when angry, or become pale when frightened.

The tree-dwelling Jackson chameleon has very interesting eyes. Mounted in little turrets, its eyes rotate separately in all directions. One can look up while the other looks down. When it spies a likely meal, however, the lizard focuses both eyes on the target. This helps the reptile to judge distance and to aim its tongue at exactly the right spot. The creature's tongue is incredibly long for its size, in fact. It's about one and a half times the length of the animal, not counting the tail. The slim, hollow tongue is pleated very tightly around a bone in the throat. When the chameleon spots an insect, tiny muscles squeeze the tongue forward in a lightning-fast strike to snatch up its prey.

The brightly colored Jackson chameleon
can change colors right on the spot.

The Nine-Banded Armadillo

Imagine an animal with a nose like a pig's, ears like a donkey's, and the shape of an armor-covered football. This is the incredible nine-banded armadillo, the only armadillo that lives in North America. A good swimmer, it crossed the Rio Grande River from Mexico and settled in Texas sometime during the last century. Since then, it has slowly spread through much of the southeastern United States, from Florida to South Carolina.

Most of the nine-banded armadillo's close relatives live in Central and South America. They each have some amazing traits. For protection, the three-banded armadillo can roll itself into a tight ball, just like a pill bug. The giant armadillo of South America has size on its side. It weighs up to 130 pounds and is about five feet long. The nine-banded armadillo can't curl up into its armor, and only weighs about fifteen pounds, but it has a startling feature all its own. In each litter, this animal always gives birth to *four* babies— no more, no less. Incredibly, the babies are always of the same sex. One year it might give birth to four males, the next year four females.

This strange-looking mammal is a burrower. It digs and roots for its food, which includes beetles, termites, worms, and even the ferocious fire ant. The nine-banded armadillo also digs the burrow in which it lives, and it doesn't mind sharing it with snakes, opossums, rabbits, or other armadillos. When threatened, this animal rarely attacks. It usually runs for safety. When the danger has passed, the nine-banded armadillo waddles out of its burrow to root about for a tasty fire ant or to have a comfortable roll in the mud.

The nine-banded armadillo may remind
you of a walking armored football.

The Okapi

About a hundred years ago, European explorers returning from Africa told a tale of a very strange beast called the okapi (oh·KAP·ee). Most people thought the okapi was just a legend. How could there be an animal that was as large as a mule with a very long neck, purplish coloring, and black-and-white stripes? A British explorer named Sir Harry Johnston believed the creature really existed. He searched in Africa and found some clues—but no animal. Scientists at the British Museum examined the clues and thought the mystery beast was probably related to the zebra or horse. Finally, a man named Karl Erikson sent the hide and skull of a freshly killed animal to Johnston. This proved that the okapi really existed, and it was not a horse or zebra at all, but a relative of the giraffe.

The Ituri (ee·TOOR·ee) Forest in northeastern Zaire (za·EER), Africa, is the home of the okapi. This peculiar animal is about six feet high at the shoulder and weighs up to 500 pounds. Its front legs are much longer than its hind legs. Males have tiny, fur-covered horns and are smaller than females. Both sexes have large ears, short, sleek hair, a tufted tail, and a tongue so long that the animal can lick its own ears!

Fossil evidence shows that the okapi has changed little over the last 30,000 years. It seems rare only because it is timid and difficult to capture. Also, its odd markings help it to blend in with the light and shadows of its dense forest home. Although the okapi's sense of smell is not very good, it has fine hearing. Thus, even barefoot natives have a difficult time sneaking very close to a bashful okapi before it scurries shyly away.

The shy okapi make their home in the dense forests of Zaire, Africa.

The Opossum

If you pretend to be asleep, many people say you are "playing possum." That's because this tricky little animal is known to play dead to fool an attacker. When frightened, the opossum disappears down a convenient hole or sometimes up a tree. When annoyed, it shows its teeth in a wide grin, and sometimes it will bite. (It has fifty teeth, more than any other North American mammal.) When trapped, however, the opossum will fall limply to the ground with saliva dripping from its gaping mouth. The attacker often loses interest and leaves. His playacting successful, the opossum then jumps up and runs away.

Ancestors of the opossum first roamed the Earth during the age of the dinosaurs. That makes this creature one of the oldest living mammals. It is the only marsupial that lives in the United States. Also unique to the opossum are its back paws. They each have four claw-tipped fingers and a fleshy thumb, much like a human hand. With these remarkable paws the opossum grasps and holds such objects as tree branches very well.

At birth, a baby opossum must use its excellent grip to work its way hand-over-hand through its mother's fur to her pouch. This trip of about three or four inches is quite a distance for a blind, hairless creature the size of a bee. The young stay in the pouch for about three months. Drawings sometimes show the mother with her tail curled above her and the babies hanging from it by their own tails. Youngsters never actually ride this way. When old enough, they ride on their mother's back, hanging onto her fur with their tiny paws.

When trapped, the North American opossum
will fall to the ground and play dead.

The Pangolin

A good nickname for the pangolin (PANG·uh·lin) might be the "living pinecone," because that's what it looks like. Its body and tail are covered with wide overlapping scales. As a matter of fact, the pangolin is the only mammal with scales, and some people call it the "scaly anteater." Its scales are not the usual snake or fish scales, however. Instead, they are made of stiff hair stuck together. Some hair also grows on the creature's soft underside.

The pangolin lives in parts of Asia and Africa. It moves slowly and, like the giant anteater, it may walk with its front feet turned under to protect its sharp claws. It often walks only on its hind feet, using its wide tail for balance. If frightened, this amazing creature curls into a ball. It can roll up so tightly that it is almost impossible for an attacker to find exposed flesh. The female pangolin protects her baby by curling up around it in this way.

The nocturnal pangolin hunts only at night. It doesn't have any teeth, so it laps up ants and termites with its long sticky tongue and swallows them whole. Sometimes the armored creature even swallows tiny pebbles, which remain in its stomach and help to grind the food.

The pangolin closes its ears and nostrils when it eats so that the irritating ants don't crawl inside. But sometimes the little mammal actually raises its scales so that the ants can swarm over it. The hungry ants eat parasites on the pangolin's skin that it can't reach itself. This is an example of how animals can help each other—the ants get a tasty meal and the pangolin gets a little relief from the bothersome parasites.

The pangolin looks like a walking pinecone
and can curl into a tight ball.

The Ring-Tailed Lemur

The delightful lemur (LEE·mur) belongs to the family of animals that includes monkeys, apes, and humans, called primates. It lives in wooded and rocky areas of Madagascar, a large island off the eastern coast of Africa. Lemurs, which live in small troops of up to twenty, are usually good climbers and live in trees. But that is not true for the best known lemur, the ring-tailed lemur. During cold weather, this mammal may sun itself in the treetops, but it prefers to stay on the ground where it makes its home among the rocks and boulders. A small animal, it weighs about eight pounds and is two to three feet long from nose to tail—about the size of a large housecat.

The diet of this adorable creature is made up mainly of fruit and the leaves of the tamarind tree. It has a most unusual way of eating fruit. Holding its meal in its front paws, it bites into the juicy morsel and lifts it up so that the juice drips into its open mouth. While it feeds on the ground, the ring-tailed lemur holds its striped tail straight up. The entire fluffy tail is ringed in striking black and white, so it stands out from its surroundings. In this way, the entire group can keep sight of each other.

This lemur has a special gland in its forefeet that it uses to clean its lovely tail. In fact, the ring-tailed lemur spends a lot of time cleaning itself and combing its fur with its teeth and claws. It's hard to imagine that this well-groomed animal gets into "stink fights." During mating time, that is exactly what the normally peaceful males do. Their tail and forearm glands secrete a strong-smelling substance. Males rub the powerful scent on twigs and wave them all about.

*The ring-tailed lemur of Madagascar looks
more like a racoon than a primate.*

Sand Skinks

Now you see it. Now you don't. The light-colored sand skink of Central Florida seems to vanish instantly. If threatened by a predator, this member of the lizard family will stay very still. Blending well with its sandy environment, it hopes not to be noticed. If that doesn't work, in a few seconds the amazing little creature can wriggle down into the sandy soil and completely disappear. Like most skinks, this five-inch-long lizard has shiny, overlapping scales and a rounded body, but few other lizards have legs like those of the Central Florida sand skink. They are so small that unless you are quite close, you may not notice them at all.

People have found different kinds of skinks on every continent except Antarctica. Most members of this large family of lizards live in tropical areas. Sand skinks, however, live in pine woods or hot deserts that have dry, sandy soil. All sand skinks have extraordinary eyelids. The lower one has a clear "window" in it. Even with its eyes closed, the creature can still see as it tunnels through the sand.

The remarkable sand skink of North Africa is a desert skink. A fringe of scales on its toes keeps it from sinking and helps it to move easily over the loose sand. With its tiny legs, the North African sand skink can actually "swim" just below the surface of the desert. It's no surprise that people have nicknamed this lizard the "sandfish." It burrows along, gathering up the termites and beetle larvae on which it feeds. It has no ear openings and finds its prey by feeling for the vibrations they make when moving through the sand.

Within just a few seconds, the sand skink can vanish into the soil.

The Star-Nosed Mole

It doesn't matter much to the star-nosed mole if it is day or night, because it spends a lot of its time underground. An expert tunneler, its strong, sharp claws are turned outward at its sides to work as diggers. This mole digs through the dirt by pressing loose soil to the sides and moving it away with its hind legs. The star-nosed mole is nearly blind. It does have eyes, but they are tiny and hidden beneath its soft fur. This doesn't seem to matter to the strange animal, because it has excellent senses of smell and touch to help it find its way.

You can find the star-nosed mole in the moist soil of the marshes, streambanks, lake shores, and meadows of eastern North America. The most astounding feature of this five- to eight-inch-long animal is a fleshy disk at the end of its long snout. The disk is tipped with twenty-two short, very sensitive tentacles. This "star" is fully developed at birth and helps the mole to find food and to feel its way around inside its tunnels. When swimming or digging, it covers its nostrils with the tentacles to keep out water or dirt.

The star-nosed mole is a good swimmer and often catches tiny minnows to eat. It also eats earthworms that it finds while tunneling. Sometimes it finds more worms than it can eat at one time, so it stores them for later meals by biting off their heads so they can't crawl away. One observer found an underground chamber stocked with more than 1,200 earthworms. You may have guessed that this mole eats a lot, about its own weight every day. If you weigh 100 pounds, you would have to eat more than a hundred hamburgers a day to eat as much as a star-nosed mole.

The star-nosed mole uses its peculiar
"star" to feel its way through tunnels.

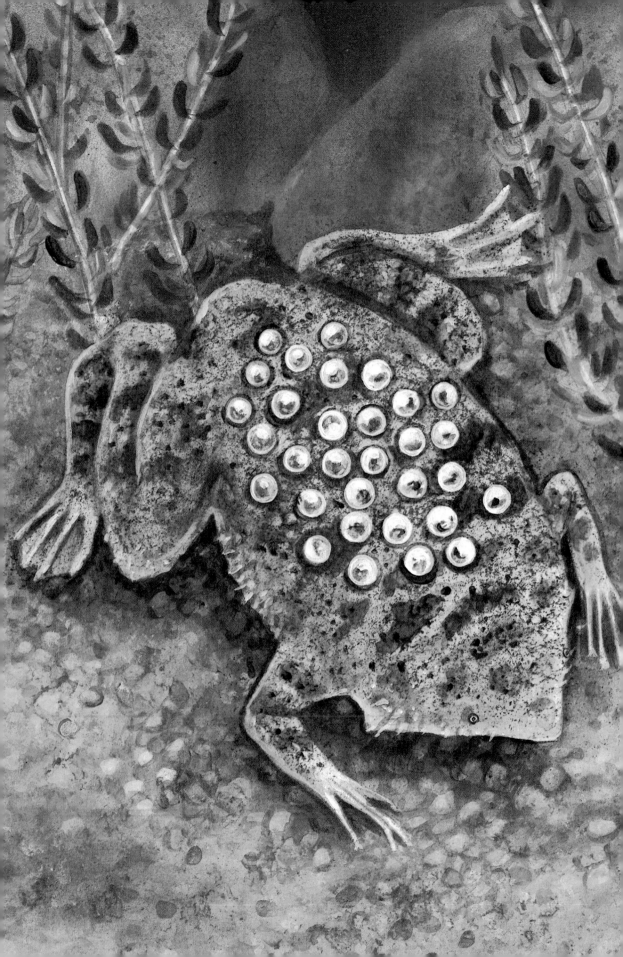

The Surinam Toad

The Surinam toad is a South American amphibian that takes its job as a parent very seriously. Not only does the female care for her young, but she doesn't go anywhere without them. During breeding season, the female lays up to 100 eggs near the water's surface. The male fertilizes the eggs and very carefully places each one on the female's back, where they stick in place. The eggs slip into small hollows that form on the female's back and are slowly covered over by a thin growth of skin. When the eggs hatch, the little tadpoles are sealed safely in these protective pockets. After they develop into tiny toads three to four months later, the mother toad rubs her back against something to scrape away the skin. Her care for her young is finally complete, and the tiny toads are freed.

This peculiar-looking toad lives on land, but unlike most toads, it captures its meals underwater. It has fringes of skin along its mouth, which attract curious fish. Most frogs and toads capture insects with their long, sticky tongues. Since the Surinam toad hunts underwater, a tongue would not be helpful, so it doesn't have one at all.

This toad has a very different method of hunting its prey. It can stay underwater for long periods. It sits quietly on the bottom of a stream with its thin fingers spread out in the mud. The animal blends into the murky bottom and is difficult to see. If a curious little creature comes close, or perhaps gently touches the toad's waiting fingers, the Surinam toad snatches it, pops open its mouth, and swallows the victim whole.

The weird-looking female Surinam toad
roosts her eggs on her back.

The Philippine Tarsier

Can you roll your eyes? The Philippine tarsier (FIL·ih·peen TAR·see·ay) can't. Its huge round eyes are fixed in their sockets, so when the little creature wants to look to one side, it must turn its entire head. While resting in the hollows of trees or clinging to vertical branches, it usually keeps one eye open. At the sound of a strange noise, it twists its ears in the direction of the noise until it finds the source, and then it slowly turns its head to look.

The name tarsier comes from the word *tarsus*, which in Latin means "ankle bone." It's easy to understand how this animal got its name–the ankle bones in its slender hind legs are unusually long. On the second and third toes are sharp claws, which it uses for grooming. The rest of the tarsier's twenty toes and fingers end in soft, flattened discs. These pads act like suction cups to help the animal hang on to tree branches.

This tarsier lives in forested areas of the Philippines but may also live on farmland. Farmers don't seem to mind, because the little animal eats insects. When hunting at night, it hops on the ground like a frog and leaps on its victim. It can leap as far as six feet in one jump. That's pretty good for a creature that is only six to eight inches long, not counting its tail. The Philippine tarsier particularly likes to eat grasshoppers and catches them in its tiny hands. It can eat thirty or forty insects at one meal. After such huge meals, it's amazing the tarsier weighs only three to five ounces– no heavier than a small bird.

The amazingly huge eyes of the tiny
Philippine tarsier are fixed in place.

The Texas Horned Lizard

The Texas horned lizard looks like a miniature version of a movie monster. Rows of pointed scales line its sides, back, and tail, and a fringe of spiky horns crowns its head. It is very fierce looking indeed. The Texas horned lizard grows up to seven inches long, which makes it one of the largest North American horned lizards. However, if it is threatened by a hungry snake or coyote, the lizard can puff itself up to seem even larger to frighten its attacker. If that doesn't work, this extraordinary animal has a more unexpected defense. When it's threatened, the horned lizard, or "horny toad," can actually burst blood vessels in its eyes and shoot a small stream of blood from the corners toward the enemy's eyes. The blood irritates the attacker's eyes, and the lizard is able to make its escape. If you ever go to the desert and try to catch the horned lizard, it may even shoot blood at you!

The Texas horned lizard probably does seem like a huge monster to the insects it gobbles up for food. Actually, this scaly reptile is harmless and quite shy. It blends well with the coarse, sandy soil of its desert home and usually relies on camouflage for defense. Its diet includes large, live ants. Most of its moisture comes from eating these insects, but it laps up dew or raindrops when it has a chance. During the hottest hours of the day, the tough little lizard hides under rocks or buries itself in the sand to escape the strong desert sun. Although this animal is a popular pet, it doesn't survive well in captivity. It thrives in climates much hotter and drier than people can provide in the home, so it should be left undisturbed in the wild.

Ready for a movie monster role—
the Texas horned lizard, or "horny toad."

The Three-Toed Sloth

Nothing about the three-toed sloth is normal. Because of two extra bones in its neck, it can turn its head almost all the way around and look behind itself. It spends most of its day thirty to ninety feet up in the treetops of Central and South American jungles, hanging by its claws. The furry sloth seldom comes down from the trees. In fact, during the rainy season, it almost looks like it's becoming a part of the tree. That's because green algae (AL·jee) grows in its fur, giving the animal a green tint. A motionless three-toed sloth, therefore, is very hard to see among the leaves.

The three-toed sloth may be one of the slowest animals on Earth. It moves hand-over-hand among the shadowy tree branches at about one mile per hour. When you think that a human walks at about three miles per hour, you can imagine how slowly the sloth moves. On the ground this animal can't walk at all and must drag itself along on its belly. It is also very difficult to pull a sloth away from its branch. Indians who hunt the creature as food usually cut the branch from the tree and carry it away with the sloth still attached.

Nine different kinds of moths and four kinds of beetles live in the sloth's fur. The peculiar animal grooms itself very slowly, so the moths and beetles are easily able to move before the sloth can snatch them up. The sloth is a good swimmer and will sometimes paddle in lakes or ponds. The insects crowd onto the animal's head and back to stay dry as they ride along.

Graceful and furry, the three-toed sloth
may be the slowest animal on Earth.

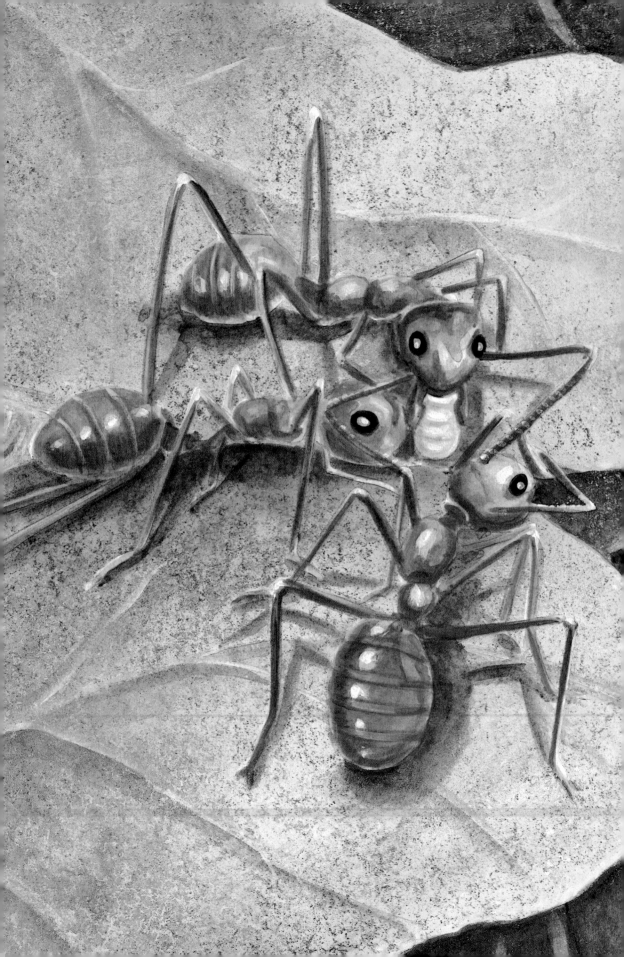

Weaver Ants

Just as people usually work together to build their homes, weaver ants work together to build their nests. Their nests are made of leaves "sewn" with silken threads that are much like the threads spiders use to spin their webs.

But adult ants don't produce silk. Where does it come from, then? Weaver ant babies, or larvae (LAR·vee), do produce silk for their cocoons, but since they're only larvae they can't move from leaf to leaf in the treetops. How is the needed silk brought to the nest? The amazing solution is a group effort. Some ants carry larvae to the nest sight, while others help create the nest. One ant grasps a leaf in its jaws and another leaf in its back claws. Then the ant pulls the two leaves as close as possible. To sew the edges together, another ant grasps a larvae in its jaws and gently squeezes it. As the little creature begins to produce a sticky silken thread, the adult ant moves the ant baby from the edge of one leaf to the next, and back again. Slowly the leaves are "sewn" together. That is why these unusual creatures are also known as tailor ants.

The weaver ant of Asia is aggressive and will attack with a painful bite. Like all insects, it has a hard outer covering called an exoskeleton (EK·soh·skel·uh·ton). Having its body support on the outside enables the ant's muscles to work more efficiently. Some ants can lift fifty times their own weight. If that were true for people, an average eight-year-old could easily lift a full-grown horse over his head.

Weaver ants use silky threads from their larvae to "weave" nest leaves together.

The Yellow-Eared Bat

The yellow-eared bat certainly wouldn't win any beauty contests. It has an odd, leaf-shaped attachment right on its nose. It is a small bat, only about two and one-half inches long, with a wingspan a little less than four inches. It weighs less than one ounce.

Bats are the only mammals that can fly. There are two main kinds, insect eaters and fruit eaters. The yellow-eared bat of Central and South America is a fruit bat. Figs, bananas, guavas, and mangoes are its favorite foods. It can eat its own weight in fruit in one evening. Fruit bats are strong fliers and may travel great distances to reach a special feeding area. The yellow-eared bat uses its keen sense of smell to detect ripe fruit in the dark. Its eyesight is also excellent, so the old saying "blind as a bat" doesn't apply here.

Bats are not fond of building shelters and usually roost in caves or trees. The yellow-eared bat is an exception. Hanging from sharp claws on its hind feet, it rests upside down during the day in tree hollows or under wide banana or palm leaves. By chewing rows of tiny holes near the centers of the leaves, the bat causes the leaf edges to droop down or fold. This forms a convenient shelter, which explains why the yellow-eared bat is sometimes called the tent bat.

A mother yellow-eared bat usually carries her single young with her wherever she goes. When she flies at night, the baby clings tightly to her fur. During the day she hugs her baby close, wrapping her wings protectively around it.

The nocturnal yellow-eared bat spends its day hanging under cool palm fronds.

The Future of Our Animals

On Earth—in our oceans and on our lands—a tremendous variety of animals is to be found. One of the greatest influences on their lives is the environments in which they live. Where an animal lives determines what it eats, where it sleeps, how it cares for its young, and even how it looks. Animals that live in a hot, dry desert need ways of obtaining and conserving water and sheltering themselves from the sun. Creatures that live in cold climates must be able to stay warm and find food during the winter months when it may be scarce.

Over hundreds of years, environments change. For example, they may become warmer, cooler, or perhaps drier. Because these shifts are usually slow, most animals can adapt to their changing surroundings. Those that cannot migrate to more suitable areas. But now humans are speeding up the process of environmental change. We dam rivers, clear away forests, and even drain swamps. Often, animals cannot adapt quickly enough to these rapid changes. For example, building a new highway or factory may destroy an animal's breeding grounds. Diverting water to a big city can remove another animal's food supply. Another way that humans change the environment is by removing predators. Wolves, great cats, and other animals considered dangerous to cattle are often destroyed. This can lead to overpopulation of the predator's natural prey. In turn, this overpopulation often leads to a strain on the food source and the animals suffer.

Of course, we must have roads, factories, and water. We must protect our crops and herds. The solution is to find a balance that will suit our needs and the needs of animals and their environments.

For Further Reading

Attmore, Stephen: *Animal Encyclopedia*, Newmarket, England, Brimax Books, 1987.

Fichter, George S.: *The Animal Kingdom*, New York City, Golden Press, 1968.

Holden, Raymond: *Wildlife Mysteries*, New York City, Dodd, Mead & Company, 1972.

McLoughlin, John C.: *The Tree of Animal Life*, New York City, Dodd, Mead & Company, 1981.

Paull, John, and Paull, Dorothy: *An Introduction to Zoology*, Loughborough, England, Ladybird Books, 1983.

Pringle, Lawrence: *Animals and Their Niches*, New York City, William Morrow and Company, 1977.

Simon, Seymour: *Strange Creatures*, New York City, Four Winds Press, 1981.

Sussman, Susan, and James, Robert: *Lies People Believe About Animals*, Niles, Illinois, Albert Whitman & Company, 1987.

Index